Libby Larsen

Fanfare for the Women

Solo trumpet in C

For the opening of the Women's Sports Pavilion at the University of Minnesota, 1993

Fanfare for the Women

Trumpet in C

LIBBY LARSEN

Fanfare for the Women LARSEN

OXFORD
UNIVERSITY PRESS

www.oup.com

ISBN 978-0-19-386007-0

9 780193 860070